G000136587

Liar Liar

by

Brian McManus

First published 2020 by The Hedgehog Poetry Press

Published in the UK by
The Hedgehog Poetry Press
5, Coppack House
Churchill Avenue
Clevedon
BS21 6QW

www.hedgehogpress.co.uk

ISBN: 978-1-913499-55-6

Copyright © Brian McManus 2020

The right of Brian McManus to be identified as the author of this work
has been asserted in accordance with the Copyright, Designs and Patents
Act 1988.

All rights reserved. No part of this publication may be reproduced,
stored in or introduced into a retrieval system, or transmitted in any
form, or by any means (electronic, mechanical, photocopying, recording
or otherwise) without prior written permissions of the publisher. Any
person who does any unauthorised act in relation to this publication may
be liable for criminal prosecution and civil claims for damages.

9 8 7 6 5 4 3 2 1

A CIP Catalogue record for this book is available from the
British Library.

Contents

The Dying Room Revisited...4

Boys Club..6

Ring of Steel 7

Casualty 8

Home Comforts 9

Call Centre 101 10

The Unravelling of Democracy.. 11

Sanitising the Jack... 12

The Awakening 13

THE DYING ROOM REVISITED

With a nod to John Gurney, my comrade in arms in the 1995 Bridport.

The Dying Room was busy, filled with noise,
the army chaps decked out in fancy dress.
With high-vis jackets, patterned shorts, the boys
the source of raucous laughter in the mess!

The flaking paint made window frames look rough,
they'd been like that since 1995.
The squaddies took their turn to spruce them up,
it made the place seem slightly more alive.

Now, engineering, plumbing, laying floors,
a different gig from fighting in Iraq,
Afghanistan, Somalia and more,
at least this time they know they're coming back.

Their grandfathers had battled on the Somme,
for them, their biggest battle lay ahead.
Their remit to ensure that nowt went wrong,
When fitting patients up for weeks in bed.

Struggling for air through their red, rubber tubes
and choking on sterile polycotton.
The nurses wet their lips with welcome ice cubes,
small kindnesses would never be forgotten.

They slip off their skins and dash across the floor
for a quick pee, an even quicker fag.
Searching for fresh gowns they find there's no more,
so they wrestle into council binbags.

The reaper doffs his cap and swings by some beds,
confirms his appointments for tomorrow.
Tells them by midday they ought to be dead,
truth be told? They don't even feel sorrow.

Every working hour they subjugate their fears,
soldiers, medics and nurses hand-in-hand.
Steadfast and sure in a valley of tears,
their mission, to prevent a new wasteland.

Shantih shantih shantih

BOYS CLUB

Their club replete with special tricks and treats
designed to keep the punters on the hook,
or on a skewer. Always tasked to meet
a certain quota, never think to look

between the layers. Press the party line,
and stay on message, don't look in their eyes.
While on the terrace, greedily they'll dine
on pain and heartache, tabloid tales and lies.

"We'll test, test, test and then we'll build, build, build!"
Results are back, we know when we've been played.
Approaching fifty thousand people killed,
Not hard to visualize *the end of days.*

Important lessons skipped, no wish to learn.
The lack of statesmanship a real concern.

RING OF STEEL

"We'll throw a protective ring of steel around all Care Homes, make sure they have everything they need." Matt Hancock

They threw a ring of steel around us, told us we'd be spared.
We toasted them with tea and buns as we sat in our chairs.
We talked of seeing friends and kids, our futures looked much brighter,
we thanked them in our prayers at night, our troubles seemed much
lighter!

Our lives limped on from day to day through feeding, pills and resting,
while worried nurses waited for their gowns and gloves and testing.
We scanned the TV news to check for signs of better weather,
it never came. Our world stayed bleak, so then we wondered whether

the bug would come. It did. The vans would hoover up the bodies.
Old Betty first then Alf then Bill and Frank, the great war squaddies.
And more would follow, nurses too and porters, maids and cleaners,
Dear Lord, they know not what they do, forgive their misdemeanours.

So now I'm lying in my box, my teeth still in a tumbler,
my dancing days behind me. Now, a never ending slumber.
You'd think they'd hang their heads in shame, their promises all busted,
Can someone ask them why, for me, their ring of steel has rusted?

CASUALTY

The scene was framed by nightclubs, cafes, bars
in days when no-one bothered where you'd go.
The bridge across the Clyde was rammed with cars,
their headlights dimmed by rain and hail and snow.

He'd light himself a fag and get a pint
in the Royal Bar, before his work.
But first get off this bridge, the weather's shite,
he slides across the slush to dodge a truck.

The waters bucked like demons in the wind,
he stretched out for a shopping trolley, failed.
Outstanding warrants, unpaid debts, he grinned,
at least the five-o couldn't get him jailed.

They wheeled him into Casualty, a mess
of blood and river debris through his hair.
Tubed him, did compressions, tried their best
to resurrect their colleague, in despair.

Did he jump or did he slip and fall?
An answer only Tommy really knows.
He turned up for the backshift after all,
beneath the sheets, a label round his toes.

HOME COMFORTS

Huddled on a bench
a binbag for a pillow
a blanket of deep, crisp snow.
I poured him some soup
he cupped his hands around it
freezing, but nowhere to go.

He lit up a fag
he'd rescued from the gutter,
offered me a draw, but I said no.
Then unstrapped his leg,
and wrapped it in his jacket,
- a roadside bomb from years ago.

I took off my scarf,
wound it round his stump,
he winced as I pulled it tight.
I threw him a mask
as he clocked the five-o
and smiled, he'd get a bed for the night.

From Helmand province
lying in a trench,
to kipping with a bug, on a city bench.

CALL CENTRE 101

CEO informs staff of Call Centre closure

The old man climbs the stairs and takes the stage,
his tired, grubby words a worthless vision
of dog-eared dogma. Ticking off each page,
the bag man and the gun moll take position

and fire. A hail of pious, sour invective
which stains the floor and curdles brittle minds.
Above, a grasping, mealy-mouthed collective
of voyeuristic palsied soldiers find

no solace in a humble mutineer
who dashes corporate plans on rocks of words.
The bag man left to choke on jeers and sneers,
the old man left to navigate the *turds.*

Despite it all the little people fall,
the corporate monolith will have its way.
The billionaire no longer owns it all,
the CEO retreats to Italy.

The gun moll gets a cheque and then a hug.
The bag man gets a cheque, that's all we're told.
The little folk now spend time with the bug,
the jury's out on whether they'll grow old.

THE UNRAVELLING OF DEMOCRACY

I sit inside this house now, filled with dread,
the networks bring the latest numbers in.
I wish they'd make up better news instead.

The stars no longer dance in blue and red,
more misery the daily bulletin.
I shut my eyes as half the world drops dead.

He topples off the mountain top. They said
he had no right of tenancy, all spin,
with nothing going on inside his head.

No elegiac spirits share his bed,
nor counsel him to wash his hands of sin.
Salvation not a path which lies ahead.

SANITISING THE JACK

The supermarket queues went round the block,
our lives were now marked out two metres squared.
The old ones stood their ground against the clock,
but truth to tell nobody really cared.

They let us in the store in dribs and drabs,
The toilet rolls were first and then the pasta.
Then heading for the checkout someone grabs
the flour out your basket. Must move faster!

The bowling club, its scattered empty chairs,
soliloquys for those not coming back.
They let us play in singles, sometimes pairs,
but first we had to sanitise the Jack.

So now we need to sanitise our world,
an acrid, broken world awash with tears.
With harrowing uncertainties now curled
like serpents' tails around us, stoking fears.

We sung and danced in 1945,
and 1953, my God, and how!
We raised the roof in 1966,
we thought it was all over, is it now?

Despite our trials and troubles, though we're numb
with grief and heartache, still we try to live
most days as if tomorrow might not come,
let's sanitise the Jack, we've more to give.

THE AWAKENING

For Jean, who suggested this poem, and lives by its principles

The bug moved in and plundered all our lives,
the certainties we cherished and enjoyed
all vanished into thin air, and contrived
to rob us of our loved ones, left a void

the size of distant galaxies, beyond
our scope for comprehension, lost in space,
we struggled to continue and respond,
normality a long-lost distant place.

But then we clapped for carers, doctors, nurses,
checked in with the neighbours, "you okay?"
Collecting tins came round, we opened purses,
let's do this then, let's live another day.

Keep close those things you value, bin the rest,
relationships and families and friends.
Let's rise up to the challenge, pass the test,
we'll make mistakes but pledge to live and learn.

To all those in the Boys Club, just a word,
watch your language, mind your p's & q's.
Your focus has been woeful, quite absurd,
you're costing folk their lives, you must improve.

It's always darkest just before the dawn,
the old days are the old days, let's move on.

Brian McManus lives on the outskirts of Glasgow with his wife and enjoys the company of his children and grandchildren who live nearby. As a former Serious Crime Squad Detective Officer Brian played a central role in the international criminal enquiry following the terrorist bombing of a Pan Am jet airliner over Lockerbie, Scotland in 1988 with the loss of 270 lives. His collection of poetry, prose and photographs recounting the events of those times was published as "Blue Daze, Black Knights – The Story of Lockerbie" in 1999. Having now stepped away from the world of work, Brian spends his time reading and writing poetry reflecting on our increasingly challenging world, and in his own small way holding to account those who abdicate their responsibility for managing it and the lack of support for those who inhabit it. "Liar Liar", his latest book of poems, are the latest sure-footed steps on Brian's very important journey, which includes other previous work published in past and pending poetry publications and online.

Upcoming poetry projects will include a major focus on the impacts of climate change on our planet and ourselves, of the near prospect of an uninhabitable earth due to intolerable temperatures and rising sea levels and all that along with the ostensible minutiae which feeds into and disproportionately affects all of our lives on a daily basis.

Staying healthy in a Covid environment presents its own challenges right across the globe and the poetry pamphlet "Liar Liar" looks closely at the impacts on the western world and in particular the UK and the USA and the dearth of both intellect and ability amongst our political leadership for managing and directing a meaningful response to such an all-encompassing disease. The increasingly rapid decline of western civilisation and the imminent threats and danger to the existing world order will form yet another investigative strand in an increasingly complex response through the medium of poetry.